REJECTED BOOKS

The Most Unpublishable Books of All Time

Graham Johnson and Rob Hibbert

bantam

All of the
authors
from the
first book
are dead.

VOODOO REPAIRMEN

BLACK MAGIC WITH WHITE GOODS

REJECTED

You can't see their faces at all!

DONALD GLOVER

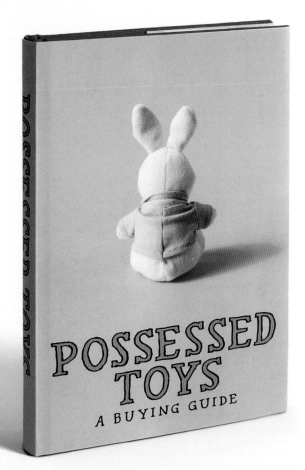

POSSESSED TOYS
TOYS
A BUYING GUIDE

A backup of
the internet
is actually
a good idea.

But the
postage costs
wouldn't make
it viable.

THE INTERNET
A HARD COPY

COOKING

FOR ~~ONE~~ *Losers*

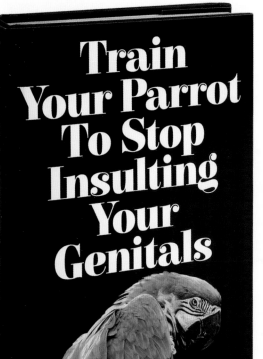

Train Your Parrot To Stop Insulting Your Genitals

DIY GLORY HOLES

REJECTED

BALLOON ANIMALS MADE EASY

THE SNAKE

THE PIG

THE ALBINO PIG

ROADKILL

Unalphabetized Dictionary

Every word in the English language, organized from best to worst

OWLS
IN FAMOUS
PEOPLE
MASKS

THE BASICS
OF SPYING

This is a
good idea,
isn't it?

RHETORICAL QUESTIONS ANSWERED

Q42 Does a bear shit in the woods?

Before we can begin to answer this question, we first need to examine the definition of 1. "a bear" and 2. "the woods."

A **bear** is a carnivorous mammal of the family Ursidae. There are eight bear species— the brown bear, the Asian black bear, the American black bear, the sun bear, the sloth bear, the spectacled bear, the giant panda, and the polar bear. The Australian koala bear is not actually a bear. They are not placental mammals but rather marsupials, so where they poop is of no consequence.

A **wood,** also referred to as a forest, is defined as an area of land covered with closely/densely packed trees.

Bamboo, however, is technically a grass, defined as an evergreen perennial from the grass family Poaceae. So whether one can call a bamboo forest a "wood" is debatable. And since **panda bears** live in thick bamboo forests (and subsist almost entirely on bamboo), exactly "where" one can say that they shit remains a matter of conjecture.

YES

Brown bear　　Asian Black bear　　American Black bear　　Sun bear

Does a polar bear shit in the woods?

No. A polar bear DOES NOT shit in the woods. It shits on the tundra of the Arctic Circle. There exists however, a grizzly-polar bear hybrid (sometimes referred to as a grolar bear, a pizzly bear, a grizzlar, or a nanulak). Because these hybrids are so rare in the wild*, the gathering of samples is extremely challenging. Zoologists estimate that there are only eight (excluding those in captivity), and that most if not all of them live in caves in the Canadian Arctic. The question here is, do they shit in their caves or do they shit out on the tundra? Either way, we can safely assume that it is unlikely that they would wander off to "the woods" to take a **dump**.

* *The grizzly-polar bear hybrids that live in captivity, obviously DO NOT shit in the woods. They shit in the zoo.*

TECHNICALLY NO   **NO**

Sloth bear   Spectacled bear   Giant Panda   Polar bear

REJECTED

Terrible
is right.

Horse in a disco

Horse with a far away lion

This will alienate
Argentinians,
the left-leaning English,
miners, anyone with
a social conscience,
and those with
a gluten allergy.

THATCHER
in the RYE

Beekeeping

How
to Keep
a Bee

REJECTED

FAMOUS
OWLS
WITHOUT
MASKS

WHERE'S WALDO?

ADVANCED

REJECTED

WINNING
TACTICS
FOR
CONNECT ONE

One-in-a-row in any direction

One-in-a-row
upward

One-in-a-row
downward

One-in-a-row
diagonal SE to NW

One-in-a-row
diagonal NW to SE

One-in-a-row
left to right

One-in-a-row
right to left

One-in-a-row
diagonal NE to SW

One-in-a-row
diagonal SW to NE

Honing your strategy

1. Win the toss

A key to winning Connect One is the ability to grasp the concept of going first.

If deciding who should go first by a coin toss, it is crucial to win. If you do not have access to a double-headed coin, make it best out of three, best out of five, etc., until you win.

REJECTED

Unfortunate

Gluing

Accidents

Where Have All
Our Forests Gone?

A report in 25 volumes

#20: Indo-Burma

Where Have All
Our Forests Gone?

A report in 25 volumes

#4: West Africa

Where Have All
Our Forests Gone?

A report in 25 volumes

#8: Indonesia

Where Have All
Our Forests Gone?

A report in 25 volumes

#12: Madagascar

Where Have All
Our Forests Gone?

A report in 25 volumes

#21: Sundaland

Where Have All
Our Forests Gone?

A report in 25 volumes

#5: Eastern Europe
Forest Steppe

Where Have All
Our Forests Gone?

A report in 25 volumes

#18: The Congo

Where Have All
Our Forests Gone?

A report in 25 volumes

#7: Philippines

Where Have All Our Forests Gone?

A report in 25 volumes

#1: The Amazon

COOKING WITH
BREAST MILK

TITAMISU

METHOD

MAKE BREAST MILK CREAM
To make 1 cup of heavy cream, mix 2/3 cup of breast milk with 1/3 cup melted butter.

MAKE MASCARPONE
Heat the cream to 185°F (stirring).

Remove from heat until it reaches 140°F.

Replace on heat again to 185°F and add the lemon juice.

Remove from heat and bring down the temperature to 140°F.

Pour the cream into a glass bowl, cover, and completely cool.

Pour into a tea towel-lined sieve and refrigerate for 24 hours.

MAKE TITAMISU
Step 1) – Make the Espresso coffee. Add 2 tablespoons of rum then set aside and let it cool.
Separate egg whites from yolks in order to whip the egg whites pretty stiff.

Step 2) – You'll know the egg whites are ready if they stay in place when you turn the bowl over. When ready, set aside.

Step 3) – Now in another bowl, whisk the egg yolks with the sugar until pale and smooth, 3 to 5 minutes.

Step 4) – When ready, add mascarpone cheese.

Step 5) – Whisk the cream slowly with the electric mixer. Now add stiffened egg whites.

Step 6) – Mix with a wooden spoon, from bottom to top. Mix slowly until it's smooth and creamy.

Step 7) – Quickly dip the Savoiardi Ladyfingers into the coffee. Cookies should not absorb too much coffee, otherwise your Titamisu will turn out too soggy. Then place them in a ceramic or glass cooking dish.

Step 8) – Spread the mascarpone cream on top of the cookies.

Step 9) – Add another layer of cookies and then cover with more mascarpone cream.

Step 10) – Finally sprinkle with cocoa powder. Let rest 3 hours in the refrigerator before serving. Add chocolate flakes on top.

INGREDIENTS

Mascarpone
Breast milk
Butter
Lemon

Titamisu
300ml of coffee
2 tablespoons of rum
4 medium eggs
100g of sugar
500g mascarpone cheese
300g Savoiardi Ladyfingers
Unsweetened cocoa powder
Chocolate flakes

The Girl
with the
Dragon Tattoo
Removed

REJECTED

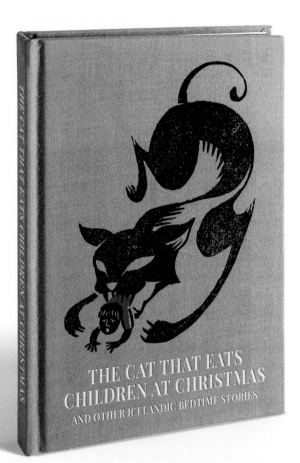

THE CAT THAT EATS
CHILDREN AT CHRISTMAS
AND OTHER ICELANDIC BEDTIME STORIES

MAKING
GOLF
INTERESTING

Bogey
monster

(Quick)sand trap

H

It's
Rough
in a
minefield

Not
Fairway

(Quick)san

Tee

FORE
fuck's sake,
exploding
rabbits

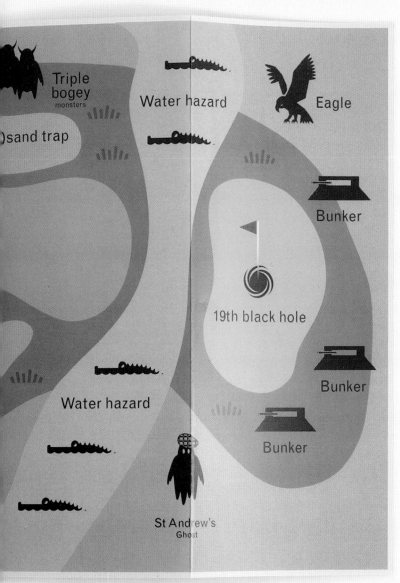

REJECTED

If you're going
to do camel toes,
you'll have to do
moose knuckles as well.

CAMEL TOES
THROUGH HISTORY

REJECTED

A beginner's
guide to
passive aggression

Read it immediately,
you fuck

REJECTED

CHECK YOUR CHILD'S IQ
CONFIRM YOUR WORST SUSPICIONS

REJECTED

HOW
TO
BURY
A
CLOWN

HOW TO BURY A CLOWN

HOW TO REALLY DRESS UP LIKE HARRY POTTER

BUILD YOUR OWN
SAND DUNE

ISSUE ONE
GRAIN ONE

REJECTED

PRANKS
WITH
SAUSAGES

REJECTED

THE SCULPTORS WHO
COULDN'T DO HANDS

EXTREME
LAWN MOWING

Now with Nude Pruning Tips

REJECTED

FLOWER ARRANGING

FOR THE IMPATIENT

REJECTED

FAMOUS FIRST ATTEMPTS IN HISTORY

#3: THE TROJAN SNAKE

REJECTED

How well
would they grip?

REJECTED

YOGA

THE SHITTEST MARTIAL ART

E.T. THE ADULT YEARS

Roma Giannino, 23

REJECTED

ANSWERS FOR MULTIPLE CHOICE EXAMS

E	C	A	C	D	A	A	D	B	A	B
C	A	C	E	C	A	C	E	A	D	D
B	C	A	C	C	B	D	C	C	A	C
E	E	C	A	B	C	A	B	B	D	D
A	C	A	C	E	A	E	B	C	B	C
E	D	B	C	A	C	A	C	A	A	B
B	C	B	A	E	E	D	B	B	E	C
E	C	A	C	B	C	A	C	A	A	A
B	C	A	C	C	B	D	C	C	A	C
E	E	C	A	B	C	A	B	B	D	D
A	C	A	C	E	A	E	B	C	B	C

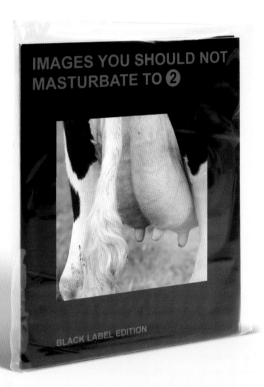

ACKNOWLEDGMENTS

Special thanks/R&D: Robyn McLellan, Edie McLellan, Sid McLellan, Lynn Johnson, Paddi Milner, Max Reed, Harry Webster, Britt Manning, Ben Grant, Pat Sofra, Mark Jones, Gav O'Brien, Eric Benitez, and anyone on your side of the fence!

Also by the same authors

Images You Should Not Masturbate To | Tarcher Perigee, 2011

How to Talk Australians web series | youtube.com/c/HowToTalkAustralians

The Elsewhere Trading Co. online store and curious prints | elsewheretrading.co

CREDITS

Concepts and sculpture-and-toast-wrangling by Graham Johnson and Rob Hibbert unless otherwise noted.

VOODOO REPAIRMEN Art direction: Natalie Johnson

FAMOUS PEOPLE IN OWL MASKS Concept: Sid McLellan

POSSESSED TOYS iStock.com/Paopano

COOKING FOR LOSERS iStock.com/Jamesmcq24

DIY GLORY HOLES iStock.com/Valeriy_G

RHETORICAL QUESTIONS ANSWERED Evgeny Turaev/Shutterstock; chempina/Shutterstock; kuarmungadd—stock.adobe.com; Carlos—stock.adobe.com; Engdao—stock.adobe.com; Kimo—stock.adobe.com; Photocreo Bednarek—stock.adobe.com; pornsawan— stock.adobe.com; New Africa—stock.adobe.com; iStock.com/tjommy; iStock.com/musat; iStock.com/Phichaklim1; iStock.com/Cody Linde

UNFORTUNATE GLUING ACCIDENTS iStock.com/g-stockstudio

COOKING WITH BREAST MILK iStock.com/SolStock

CHECK YOUR CHILD'S IQ Photographer: Matt Stoddart; talent: Freddie Stoddart

HOW TO BURY A CLOWN Art direction: Carol van Reese and Tony Rogers; photographer: Hugo Kohlerr

PRANKS WITH SAUSAGES Concept: Andrew Davies

THE SCULPTORS WHO COULDN'T DO HANDS iStock.com/221A

FAMOUS FIRST ATTEMPTS IN HISTORY: #3 THE TROJAN SNAKE faestock—stock.adobe.com; Lunstream—stock.adobe.com; Max—stock.adobe.com

AMATEUR BIRD-WATCHING Concept: Matt Stoddart

DIY BIKE RACKS Kei Uesugi/Stone via Getty Images; Juanmonino/E+ via Getty Images

E.T. THE ADULT YEARS Talent: Romy Johnson

REJECTED
BOOKS

TRANSWORLD PUBLISHERS
Penguin Random House, One Embassy Gardens,
8 Viaduct Gardens, London SW11 7BW
www.penguin.co.uk

Transworld is part of the Penguin Random House group of companies
whose addresses can be found at global.penguinrandomhouse.com

REJECTED
BOOKS

Penguin
Random House
UK

First published in Great Britain in 2022 by Bantam
an imprint of Transworld Publishers

Design by Graham Johnson and Rob Hibbert

A CIP catalogue record for this book
is available from the British Library.

ISBN 9781787636453

Printed in Italy by L.E.G.O. S.p.A

The authorized representative in the EEA is Penguin Random House Ireland,
Morrison Chambers, 32 Nassau Street, Dublin D02 YH68.

Penguin Random House is committed to a sustainable
future for our business, our readers and our planet. This book
is made from Forest Stewardship Council® certified paper.

REJECTED
BOOKS

MIX
Paper from
responsible sources
FSC
www.fsc.org
FSC® C018179

1